ST. SEBASTIAN'S PLACE

Also By T.S. Curtis

Poetry
Heart & Healing
Shades of Blue
Let Them Stare

Novels
Ink & Crown

ST. SEBASTIAN'S PLACE

T.S. CURTIS

ST. SEBASTIAN'S PLACE Copyright © by T.S. Curtis. All rights reserved. No part of this book may be used or reproduced in any manner whatsoever without written permission except in the case of brief quotations embodied in articles and reviews. For information, contact T.S. Curtis, tscurtiswriter@gmail.com

FIRST EDITION PAPERBACK

Cover photo and art © 2024 T.S. Curtis

ISBN 978-1-7779995-6-8

For Solveig.
Who heard me screaming
and didn't stop to ask questions,
just decided we were in it together.
Love ya <3

Canada
Suicide Prevention Line: 1-833-456-4566
Eating Disorder Help Line: 1-866-633-4220
Kids Help Phone (accessible up to age 29): 1-800-668-6868
Support for BIPOC people: healingincolour.com
Talk4Healing Helpline for Indigenous Women: 1-855-554-4325

Provincial Abuse Lines
    BC VictimLinkBC: 1-800-563-0808
    AB Alberta Abuse Helpline: 1-855-443-5722
    SK Mobile Crisis 24/7 Helpline: 306-757-0127
    MB Domestic Abuse Crisis Line: 1-877-977-0007
    ON Assaulted Women's Helpline: 1-866-863-0511
    ON Male Survivors 24/7 Line: 1-866-887-0015
    ON French Fem'aide 24/7 Support Line: 1-877-336-2433
    QC Bilingual SOS violence conjugale 24/7: 1-800-363-9010
    NB Crossroads for Women 24/7 Crisis Line: 1-844-853-0811
    NS Neighbours, Friends and Families (Abuse and Violence Support Line): 1-855-225-0220
    PEI Island Help Line: 1-800-218-2885
    NL Sexual Assault Crisis and Prevention Centre 24/7 Support and Information Line: 1-800-726-2743
    NWT Help Line: 1-800-661-0844
    NU Kamatsiaqut Nunavut Helpline: 1-800-265-3333

United States
Suicide Prevention Line: 988
Eating Disorder Help Line: 1-800-931-2237
Support for BIPOC people ('Call Blackline'): 1-800-604-5841

Trigger Warning

The poems in this collection deal directly with a number of heavy topics, many of which can be hard to read about, or can spark other conversations
There are poems that deal with: mental illnesses, religion and religious trauma, physical and psychological partner abuse.

On the page opposite is a list of places you can reach out to for help if you are struggling with any of these things.

My dearest reader,

When I started to fall apart
Too young to even really understand what that meant
Pages became my escape
I opened my heartbreak
And my broken soul
And tried to trace my broken body onto a page
And so many people told me
They hated poetry
And would never pick up my book
No matter how much they liked me
I don't write for them
I write for those
Still trying to find their escape
So if that is what has brought you here,
Welcome to St. Sebastian's place
For loners, and different, and all of us still trying
To piece ourselves together
All are welcome
I'm happy you decided to join us

    - Tegs

TABLE OF CONTENTS

GROUNDED..1

Growing Old..3
Once And Heart..4
Eulogizing, Prophesizing..5
Where The Poems Came From..6
Fake Politics...8
Homebound..9
Home, Again..10
Jack In A Box...11
I'm Sorry..12
Stop Motion Memories..14
280 Characters...15
Happy Birthday..16
Milestones..17
Too Much Not Enough Of The Time.................................18
They Said I Owed Them An Explanation..........................19
I Can Be Enough..20
I Told You..21
Secrets (I Told You Part 2)...22
Held (I Told You Part 3)..23
Wuthered..24
Movie Theatres..25
In A Heartbeat...26
16 Lashings..27
Storm Loves..28
Moss Grown Words..29
Could Have Been..30
My Favourite Metaphor..31
This Will Be Rewritten...32
A Writer's Burden...33
The Author's Note..35
The Story Collector's Warning...36
Always The Writer, Never The Muse...............................37

MAYDAY..**39**
Fingers..41
Divine Right...42
Avenue Club..43
That Love...44
Sweet Tooth...45
Library, Room J...46
Track 3...47
Broken Record Players, Dusty Shelves.........................48
My Phone Makes Too Many Noises.............................49
Who Needs Receipts? 50
Replies..51
Broke Again...52
Comfort Films...53
Crinkled Roads..55
Handsome Cabs on Silt Roads.......................................57
Steering Wheel...58
Crinkled Roads Pt. 2...59
Why Do You Ask? 60
The Devil Wore Grey..61
Apple Tree..62
Cowardice..64
Rocks..65
Perfect Storm...65
Final Shade of Blue...67
Choices Pt. 2..69
Love Me Not Or Never..70
An Ode To My Own Karma..71
Wax and Wane...72
The Little Fairy Tales..73
Rotten 74
Wrong Time...75
A Drive Through the Rubble of Mother Nature's Fury........76
Mourning Sun..77
The Ancients..78
Your Hand..79

ROOTHEAD 81
Graduate 83
St. Sebastian's Place 84
I Am Not A Church Pew 87
Falling With Grace 88
Quies 89
My Peace 90
Perfect 91
A Home For The Next 92
Safe Spaces 93
Still Here 94
Still Here Pt. 2 95
Clockwork (Still Here Pt. 3) 96
All those Epic Loves 97
Sue, Misrule, and Patchouli 98
Fairy Woords 100
Putting Down Tracks 101
It's Okay To Be An Ending 102
Mending (Or: Blurry October) 103
The Recovering Memory 104
For The Broken Little Girls 106
Why I Stopped Caring What Others Said 107
Why I Am More Careful With What I Say 109
Lips Moving 111
You Did Not Manifest This, I Promise 112

THE CANON 113
The Saints of This Place 115
Abandoned Place of Worship 116
Historical Notes 117
Until Safer Tides 119
Softly (An Ode to St. Francis) 121
St. Atwood 122
August 123
Joan 124
St. Gobnait 125
St. Rita 126
The Miller 127

Little Girls, Bloodied Fingers...129
The Robin 130
To Love Again..131
St. Isidore 132
Lament to St. Lidwina...133

Disclaimer..135

Your Turn..137

T.S. Curtis

GROUNDED

St. Sebastian's Place

Growing Old

We were so afraid
Of growing up
Destroying ourselves to fit
The things we thought
And thought wrong

I can't wait to be
The lady
Who sits with lines on her face
From years of smiling
Leaving kindness wherever I go
Wisdom lingering
From a life
I built

Because growing old
Is a privilege
Even if it's on my own
And I have already missed too much of this life

Once And Heart

To all those we had to leave behind
In the past lives
Etched on our hearts
Even when the memories try to fade
Every part of who we become
Has a little piece
Of who you were

Eulogizing, Prophesizing

The speaker told us
To write a eulogy
Said it convinced to live life to the fullest

But those of us who spent our lives
Wanting to die
Saw the end of our life
As an ending
And writing them
Was an ending

I don't care what the page says at the end
What others remember over a grave
This is my here and now
I can only know the pieces that make me happy
Without hurting any more

Where The Poems Came From

A circle of chairs in back rooms at event halls
    they told us they don't normally rent out
    too small to contain their usual crowds
Church basements we share with
    Girl Guide groups and
    Alcoholics Anonymous
    And we're all just looking for connection in each other
Empty coffee shops with tiny raised platforms
    the usual patrons avoiding the *Poetry Night* sign at the door
Dishevelled second-hand bookshops
    the floor bowing under the weight
    of the trauma of the half dozen poets gathered there
    as we spill broken fragments of words into each other's laps
    spending the night trying to arrange them into something
    we can recognize

Our poems have always
Been a way
Of recognizing
What's broken
And jumbled
On the inside

The poems are for us
Not for you
If we find comfort in others words
That's the beauty of being human
What has been one
Has been all

The art is not in the rhyme
But the divine way
We leave our souls on the ground and hope someone sees us

We learned their rules
But when we grew tired of the sonnets
And the rhymes in the limericks became too overwhelming

T.S. Curtis

For the stories we tried telling
We took the poems back
It was our turn
And maybe screaming into a microphone was all we needed

Because as long as it was said
In a way that people would remember
And could stuff their hands through the words to find connection
Where is the harm in new poems
That have new rules
Or no rules at all

I told them
That the story
Lived inside us
If they were only willing
To listen
-*t.s.c.*

St. Sebastian's Place

Fake Politics *(An Ode to uOttawa Model Parliament)*

It's hard to say goodbye to something
That no one else quite understands
Where we joke that everything is fake
But it has always felt safe

To the people who I sometimes
Only know by place

The politics may have been fake
But everything else I felt
Was real

T.S. Curtis

Homebound

Learning to live
In the hometown that I fled
Has been harder
Than learning to find an embrace in
The city that never felt like home

Home, Again

I told you that I missed
The only place we'd both called home
That I'd lost a piece of my soul
And wished I could just feel like I was whole again

You asked me for my address
For the palace that's been my in between
And for a split second I remembered
The only love letter you ever sent
But on Christmas morning
I found
A jar in a box filled with pebbles
And sand
And to everyone else it may seem
Like a silly gift
A forgotten last minute thing

But to me
You tried
To bring me home

T.S. Curtis

Jack In A Box

Growing up
In a town
Where your identity
And thoughts
Are called wrong
Is hammering yourself into a box
And feeling like a traitor
While trying to mince your words
Having to agree
Because you've watched them
Destroy people
And you're only twenty-two
You can't afford
The ruin
That they represent
And you know
That you will never get to truly be you
And you just wish they would see you
And let it be
Because they will always get to be them
And you will always be some fractured reflection of
The *them*
They made you out to be

St. Sebastian's Place

I'm Sorry

I'm sorry you've forgotten
What I sound like
And that I don't remember how to hug you
And that my hands shook

I'm sorry I retreated inside of me
Pushed the world
And all its people
Out of my own little world

There's just a lot going on
Right now
And I can't find the words
To explain to you
That I'm somewhere
Between depressed

And growing again

.
.
.

I danced around the kitchen last week
I talk to my cat like he's human
And that might be ridiculous
But I say the words out loud
And the sound of my voice
Is breathing life into some part of me
That had shut the door where I had retreated
Left in storage for when I could feel like me again

I didn't know if me was in me anymore

Two years was hard

I'm in here

T.S. Curtis

I'm coming home to me

No need to apologize.
Just knock.

Stop Motion Memories

I may not remember much
Holes scattered across my memory
But I do remember
The first time we landed at an airport in a new city
Took a car down the road and I still have the loops and the view memorized
And the tunnel
A tunnel with too many lights
Stop motion over your face
And I tried to draw patterns with the freckles on your nose
I don't remember what we talked about
But I do remember how you laughed
And how it always filled your whole face
Until your dad made it something you thought was bad
And you'd hide it

We were too young for me to know
Those feelings of falling for you
But deep down
Watching you in stop motion
And memorizing the freckles on your nose
Felt like love
Even if it took me five years too late
To realize

T.S. Curtis

280 Characters

Every few months
I open her Twitter
My fingers know her handle by heart
To quietly scroll through her mind
And remember
What we were
Expertly avoiding the like button
As she walks down the street in bright eyeshadow
Telling me short stories on a screen
Like she once told me in person
When we were both too scared to say our alphabet out loud
Even when one little letter could have told her who I am
And yet eight little letters could never fully describe
How I felt about her
When she sat beside me
To silently wipe my tears
Holding me together
Until it was her that tore apart
And her Twitter is full of words
Like those that I remember
Strung together like the poems I wanted to write for her
And I am so lucky to
Have known her once
And watch forever from afar
She doesn't need my 'like'
She will always have a piece of my heart
This love has become different

But never any less

Happy Birthday

It's so strange
To get a Facebook notification
To wish your best friend happy birthday
When you haven't said
Hello
In seven years
And you don't really know
What happened
You just know
That you miss them
And that you wonder every day if they miss you
After you agreed that
Seven years meant
Forever
And I just kept falling in love with them

Do you say happy birthday?

I ex out the notification

Milestones

I wonder what it is
To walk through life
With the same people who have always been there
Old friends
Who never become new friends
Contact books
That don't need updating
Pages torn out
To make way
For the new adventures
Always coming back
To the same people
Each stage of life
Shared
Standing up at milestones
To recount old memories
Because you were there for all of them
From the first ones
Childhood photos and stories
Not just part of my history
But my once and now and future
Never having to *what's your name? Favourite colour?*
Not watching a life from afar
Phone calls before Facebook updates
Will I be the only one left for my milestones

Too Much Not Enough Of The Time

A promise to not be alone
Banks on others taking up the mantle with you
You meter yourself
Never sure when talking
Too much
Is too much
But you haven't been social enough
And you promised your mom not to isolate
And you're out
And about
And alone
Again
I told you everything
Spilled the soul to the questions
You came up with
Volleyed
So you felt heard
This would be a two way stream
I would not let us be alone here

I'm glad you have found your people

Here's to trying to find mine
Again

T.S. Curtis

They Said I Owed Them An Explanation

How do you explain
When half of it got washed away under restless rain
And the scars and bruises are only on the inside

I Can Be Enough

It's too much to love you
If they can't hold you in their two hands
Or count your achievements on their fingers

Why do I have to fit into their box
And they can't grow to fit into mine

T.S. Curtis

I Told You

When you told her things
And you wanted her to hear you
But she never seemed to
And instead
Told over you

So you stopped telling

Pick and choose
And told her
Make it all acceptable
Everything stuffed into your throat

Let bite sized pieces
Out through the grapevine
Only to tell you it's not true
And you can't scream
And tell her how much she'll never know

So you suck back the anger

Hide the hurt away
And nod
And she'll never know
And she'll never know she hurt you
By never stopping to
Listen

Secrets (I Told You Part 2)

I told you
Glitter glued to our face
Moon shining off the water
Alone on the beach
After hours of feeling accepted

I told you that night
But that did not
Make it
Your secret
To tell

T.S. Curtis

Held (I Told You Part 3)

I couldn't tell you
I wanted to say it
On my time
In my way
But their mouth tore me apart
Before mine could
I don't know whose fault it is now

Wuthered

The thorns didn't matter
The honeysuckles wrapped me in
And I convinced myself that was enough

T.S. Curtis

Movie Theatres

I love the movies
I'm a wait in line for
Butter in the middle and on top
Settle into always slightly uncomfortable chairs
Too deaf to catch every word
Lover of the movies
Seven times over the first
In line for Marvel movies that always managed to coincide with my birthday

I've never loved a movie more than
When you sat next to me
For the first time
Our backs pressed together
Fingers tripping together in fear
First I showed you my favourite
The first time you kissed me was to your favourite
And our favourite was in a crowded theatre
Hands wrapped together
I still remember my blue shirt
And your stark red

I'm at another marvellous movie now
You're a half a lifetime away
And I hope there's a universe
Where we got to watch
This one together

St. Sebastian's Place

In A Heartbeat

Careful when you hand an artist your heart
And break theirs
We may not ruin your life
But we'll tell the world how you ruined ours
Without ever having to utter your name again

T.S. Curtis

16 Lashings

Everything we did
Was a choice by the end of his fingers

And his words lashed across my cheek
Every time he blamed me for what we did
What he asked
And pushed

By his hand
It was my fault

And no one has been allowed to touch me since

Storm Loves

Some small loves aren't meant to last
But like a storm passing through
They come to heal
Bring new life back to the dry ground
Fresh air rustling the leaves and shaking out the dust
Nurturing the roots inside our souls
So that we can grow from those who left us broke

A coming apart is not always a crack
Or a rip
Or a sever
But a gentle step
An understanding

Even if we weren't forever
You put the air back in my lungs

Moss Grown Words

I asked the universe
To sing me to sleep
Hold me
As the world slips through my fingers
They sent me you
Plucking strings
To a moss-covered song

Could Have Been

As you led me through the unknown
The tree branches caressing my cheeks
You turned around
Checking I was here
Following in your footsteps
The squeeze of a hand
The silent I Love Yous
I didn't disappear
But we did
Slowly
Maybe you never should have
Looked back for me
That love
In checking I was there
I was with you
I was okay
Was all that mattered

T.S. Curtis

My Favourite Metaphor

You'll always be at the bottom
Of my double meanings
Whether we like it or not
We always have the words
We left each other

This Will Be Rewritten

Do you rewrite
The ways we were
The way I did
Wrote the love and hope
The crossed fingers it wasn't me
Fingers crossing for it to get better
Some Days
and Always
Replacing the venom
Do I write to forget
Do I write to remember
Do I write to hope
Do I start them again
Rewrite them edged in the venom you left
In the cracks you broke
Maybe it was always about hope
Maybe the poems
Were never for you
Poems for me
Holding the pieces that could be
Survival woven between the lines
Written into pages
Torn into bandages
This is how we keep going
Let it bloom

T.S. Curtis

A Writer's Burden

My words found paper because there was no one to listen
Even at eleven I felt like I couldn't breathe
I decided too young that people found me annoying
And didn't want to hear me speak
I wrote down any thoughts and feelings
And passed them on to broken girls
With sharp edges
And made them strong
My proxies
Shells
Of women
I could become

I became a writer
To be quiet
Told I was too loud
And talked too much
And had too much to say
And was too much of a burden to be friends with
I am a writer
To fold myself
Into the pages
And try to make every other part of me
Palatable for the rest of the world

My best friend at twelve
Told me not to spend too much time with her because I was too much
There was too much burden in my words
I've spent a decade balancing the world for the oxygen I pulled
Years of quiet quiet
To let my excitement run empty
I run my friendships on a timer
So that they won't hit an expiry

I told stories and woes to myself
Because who else would listen
I was my own comfort

St. Sebastian's Place

But 12 stories
16 main characters later
I'm still trying to find someone
Who will hug me
When the story
Is over
Because words on a page
Will only keep me warm
When I light them on fire
And I'm not sure I'll ever
Be fully ready to let them go

T.S. Curtis

The Author's Note

I always read the
Author's Note first
Read the secrets that make the writer
Make the book
Make the story
Make the poems
Make the metaphors
Make it more than words on a page
So it lasts a lifetime
Extends forever away
From the fingers of the author
What was ours
Is now yours
Read carefully
Hold gently

St. Sebastian's Place

The Story Collector's Warning

Don't become a storyteller
Every moment is forever
Committed to memory
The words
Dropping through your veins
Movies are little more
Than choreography to be studied
And not enjoyed
The world becomes a palate
And you are a bank
Story tellers
Story collectors
The burden can be heavy

T.S. Curtis

Always The Writer, Never The Muse

I've written poems about you
Little poems in collections
And letters never sent
Waiting in the box that is hidden in the spot in my room
That had once been the place that I cried over
People who had left me broken
And the broken pieces have given me words
That I've given away
Sometimes I wonder if I'm worth a song
My muse, your music
First six strings, then dozens of ivory keys
Melodies abounding
And filling my soul
But never one written for me

Will I ever be a muse

Will the way I see the good in people around me
And the way I fall in love
Be enough
To give me my own little piece of
Someone else's soul
Fill the little holes
I carved out of me
To give room for others

I think the dreams
Will always be
All I might be getting

For every artist has a muse
And when you are busy feeling
With every fibre of your being
Is there enough room left for some else to recreate you

St. Sebastian's Place

T.S. Curtis

MAYDAY

St. Sebastian's Place

Fingers

There must be spikes inside my fingers
No way to
Make an instrument
Pull at heartstrings
The way the people who dragged me through
Every heartbreak have

And I just want to let the world
Mourn with me
How you told me
'I don't want you in my life'
And that three words that were everything
Became those seven words
That broke some tiny part of me
And I have never
Been the same

Divine Right

They call themselves the good ones
Doing the divine work of a God
They say has called us broken despite
The hole in their chests where the rest of our
Hearts rest
With words we know
Have never been written or spoken
And they are happy to continue
Holding mass
           destruction
In their hands to make words their laws they don't understand
Harassing reverends
                  marching for the people
Only for them to cry out that no one else
Believes quite like they do
And who are we to determine their fate
Whoever knows what truly lies in their soul
They get what is coming
For ours is the kingdom
Of the good
And the loving

T.S. Curtis

Avenue Club

Sitting at the bar
Listening to the men beside me
Drunkenly rate the women alongside me
I don't know any of their names
And neither do they
Calling them by their hair
Or their glasses
Or "the one that looks like she has brains"
Another woman walks in
And the farthest
Tells his buddies
How he slept with her
Took her home
The things she did
The things he did to her
Talking too loud
The young bartender trying to decide if she should say something
The silent eye contact between us
When the expletives hit a little too close to home
And the young man
My age
Who doesn't know them
But joins them anyway
Talks and laughs and connects
And when he turns and asks my name
I don't look as I tell him
Not interested
Thinking about the night my grandfather asked
Why I still haven't settled down
And the shiver of all the words spoken
About me runs down my back from where they were said
Pay up and leave
Only then remembering I'm alone
In a city I barely know
His seat is empty through the window as I turn the corner away
And I can't keep looking over my shoulder

That Love

They told me I wasn't old enough
To know what love is

But now here I am older
Feeling hollow
Did it break me so badly I can't feel it
Did I ever feel it
Or is this what it feels like
What that was
What that was that broke me but filled me and made me feel so horribly
Was that something else
I don't want that
But I don't want this
I want to be
Okay
And full
And safe
And loved
Will I ever be old enough
To be over that
And feel what it is they keep telling me that it is

T.S. Curtis

Sweet Tooth

She ate honey by the spoonful
And I liked to smile with lemons between my teeth
I took my martini with a twist
And she drank anything rimmed in sugar
Tongue flicking out as she tried whatever the bartender recommended
Her tongue always dyed some ridiculous shade of the rainbow
We were always trying to hide between us

Had the kind of smile that warmed your cheeks in the winter
And always added an extra sugar cube to her tea
She was a big fan of marshmallows even when she was trying
To make s'mores in the microwave
And I was hand in hand with my black coffee
Too many cups at finals season

I've been told I put sugar between my words
Sweeten what I say until it hurts
Balance bitter with the sugar that I spit out
But she left a special little trail
Of kindness
Sweet words
And moments
And every memory tinged in clouds of cotton candy

She left

The toothache I should have expected
Because she was the first thing
That made me think I could have a sweet tooth

St. Sebastian's Place

Library, Room J

When you let go
Because you needed something sweeter
I got softer
Not out of spite
Like the ones before you had left me
Left me picking up the pieces
And glueing together sharp edges
You didn't grind down the sharpness
You made it easier to hold

You left me with the lessons
I needed to learn
We may not have been right then
But whoever we are right for
Get to have us better for
Having you and me been
Us

Track 3

You said you loved it
When I danced with you
High heels clicking
And socked feet catching on old floors
And laughter in time with the music notes
But you never took the time to
Learn the steps for me
And I can't keep tripping on the
Broken promises

Broken Record Players, Dusty Shelves

I have shuffled the deck
Too many times
To keep coming on your calling card
I don't know if you even remember giving it to me
And you've cleared out the memories
You can smile like nothing happened
And even though gentle hands
Held me better
And tender words
Made me better
Your smile is tacked to the edge of every memory
The little words I managed to get from you
On repeat
Scratching
Bumping against each other
Almost incoherent
Trying to hold on to them

T.S. Curtis

My Phone Makes Too Many Noises

Things changed when I
Stopped smiling at the buzz of
Notifications

St. Sebastian's Place

Who Needs Receipts?

When I have the poems

That's all the proof I need

T.S. Curtis

Replies

It's a lot easier
To take a rejection when it isn't
Read at 9:43 PM

St. Sebastian's Place

Broke Again

I broke again
And looked you up
And I'm so happy that you
Look like you're smiling

T.S. Curtis

Comfort Films

We've been here before
With the little videos
Playing over our screens
The only light in our dark bedrooms
Exiles across the country
When you said you wanted this
You made me promise
I would be okay
A world away from our little town
And I promised you it wouldn't
Be my undoing
And here you are unravelling

We've all been here before
Planting warning
After warning
That I should know the signs
I've seen the credits rolling
I know how this is going
I know where this road turns into
An end

I've been here before
With you breaking my heart
And a mouth full of spite
And screaming that I
Should have seen this coming
Because I know you

I know you

I probably know you all too well

I can recite the lines you wrote

And watched the way you
Let them spill
I could always read your face

St. Sebastian's Place

But never understood how to
Read the rest of you

I've never been here before
Feet still firmly on the ground
While you rushed away
Because all this time
As you side stepped around me
Saying you were doing it to protect me
I've been growing
And the tears you left me with
Are feeding the garden of my becoming

I've seen this film before

I should have guessed the ending

But I've always liked the movies

T.S. Curtis

Crinkled Roads

Lonely roads
Door handles
Pulled open too late so that our story had to hold this broken piece
And my ears would never stop with your ringing
The way the air burned my lungs
When all I had craved for months was to breathe in the place that had felt like home
A voice twisting into the wind behind me
A voice that became an unknown somewhere along the way
Unknown dirt road ahead of me
Like the time we were too lost with backpacks too heavy for our old selves
      so we left a piece of our souls out there
And here you were threatening to grab hold of a piece of mine
But not the pieces I was working to be better than
The pieces I had fought to put together
It's your voice on the wind
Insisting
      Demanding I come back

Only I freeze

This road ahead of me
I don't know it
For the second time in my life
I'm beyond lost
Every step sinks into the crinkled grime below me
Somewhere, out there, is someone who knows me
And behind me is someone I'm pretty sure never did
I could run
Down this road ahead of me
In the growing pattering of rain like some kind of freedom I used to crave even before you waltzed into the ruin of my path
Your voice softens and my hands flex and I don't want to cry in front of you
Not again
Because you know which button to push

St. Sebastian's Place

And which door to try
And which piece to balance in place
I get in the car and you flip a u-ey
And drive back up a path you seem to know
Over my sunken footprints
And erase any chance of my choice being the last one

T.S. Curtis

Handsome Cabs on Silt Roads

Standing outside
A car that was never a taxi
Screaming at me from the other seat
Trying to let myself out
Ready to walk all the way
In a place I have no directions for
Demanding I come back
To this day I still think
I never should have gotten back in

Steering Wheel

I didn't learn to drive
Because you told me it was a failure of mine

I learned to drive
So the next person who tried to grind me into the pavement
Tried to leave me relying on their ability to get me out
Can be left in my dust

T.S. Curtis

Crinkled Road Pt. 2

That winding dirt path
Eventually led me back
To me
Even if I had to unweave
The broken from my memory
To stand back

And let hearts and home claim me as their own

St. Sebastian's Place

Why Do You Ask?

They asked me to stop writing poems that were damning
I asked why they thought the poems were about them

T.S. Curtis

The Devil Wore Grey

The promise
Was that the devil would come in
Riding his horse
In tasseled robes
Bright and vicious
We would know
When the devil rode in
To steal our hope
And break our souls

But the devil wore grey
Quiet enough for the both of us
As wretched fingers wrecked this
This destroyer of hope
The devil wore grey
Unassuming
Green-eyed
The devil wore grey
Called me demon
In my pain
And my dismay
The devil wore grey
Ripped my heart out
Let the venom take a bite
The devil wore grey

And the colour bled out

St. Sebastian's Place

Apple Tree

There was an apple tree that used to hang
Over the rotting fence that had survived one too many winters
Between my home and the neighbours

Crab apples
Little balls
That fell into our yard
And melted into sticky sweet grass
Crawling with bugs
Until every piece was picked away

Every apple you bit into
Tasted different
And you had to eat each one through
To know
Whether they were sour
Or sweet
Or rotten in the core
Because rot
Doesn't always
Find its way to the surface
It's pushed down where it can linger
Break down from the inside out

There was an apple tree
Over the rotting fence that had survived one too many winters
Between mine and my neighbours
And every once in a while
I would sit beneath it
Awaiting my Isaac Newton moment
My breakthrough

And a good bonk on the head to get me going again

Until the rot hidden deep inside the trunk
Passed through and destroyed the beauty of the tree
Teetering over and leaving
A mess of rotted branches twisted together
And paint chipped from the rotting fence
And took its mysterious apples with it

Cowardice

It's a coward's way
To break a pact
Without a word
Part of loving you
Has always been waiting for
The moving on that would just be another part
Of another day
That was quiet
And kind
And I kind
Of wish I could have told you
Good luck
Or congratulations
And greeted you with a smile

But instead
You stole that
And left every supporting wall
Of our good place
In ruins of anger

T.S. Curtis

Rocks

Every word you used against me
Convinced me I was hard to love

Even I found it too hard to love me

St. Sebastian's Place

Perfect Storm

Once upon a times
Or dark and stormies
Or happily evers
At this point
I'll take whatever
Cliche
Doesn't get me hurt

T.S. Curtis

Final Shade of Blue

You were always my blue
The cool relief
From my own chaos
Bright solace in the
Grey days
And sometimes a grey mood
When you kept pushing me into a cycle
That was somewhere between cold and hard
But blue was always too good to let go of

A comfort
A favourite colour
A comfy sweater
A climbing harness
An ocean that felt like home
And an expanse of sky
That broke us apart

A book cover

But in a second
You flashed into something red
Soaked in an anger that you pulled into existence
The end of a needle
Pulling thread through the tapestry
From the depth of a place that is now just
The title of another poem written for you
That I almost want to throw into the red flames
And I never want to see blue again
Stained fingers
From crushed blackberries
On long hikes filled with laughs
Are just memories
And my next poems
Will be green
And yellow
And red

St. Sebastian's Place

And pink
And purple
And everything I never wanted to tell you
And maybe someday they will be blue
But they won't be your blue
Of a broken pen
In a broken heart
And that's okay

T.S. Curtis

Choices Pt. 2

I sometimes wonder about the choices I made
Of who I would have been
With the other boxes ticked
If I'd followed my heart the first time
If I hadn't run back to you
If I'd let you in on the secret
If the ground hadn't fallen out from under me
And found a place for my two feet
On my own

St. Sebastian's Place

Love Me Not Or Never

I asked you to tell me
That you never loved me
Not out of spite of our horrid ending but
So that every hurtful thing
You did
And said
Wasn't out of something that was
Twisting how it meant to love me
Wasn't
Twisting how I thought I should be loved

Yet somehow even at the end
You couldn't give me the one thing
I asked for
After months of asking you to love me
In a way I know I deserved
And you couldn't even tell me
You never did

T.S. Curtis

An Ode To My Own Karma

I won't say I hope you get to love
The way you deserve
Because after everything
What you deserve
What you have earned
Is not the kind of energy
I want to wish on anyone

And I believe
In the kind of love that I deserve
After everything

So for you
I hope for the kind of love
We all want

Wax and Wane

As my health waned with the
Fast coming of the new summer moon
The person he looked up to
Was just
Waiting for it to be entirely my fault
Or the Creator's
Whoever struck first
So that it wasn't her hand that squeezed the life from us
She was always ready for my mess to be destruction from chaos
Not creation
           from the chaos
To her
I was a complication
With complications
But it was I that was tied into the fold of his disaster

I think it happened in the dark
I remember steps
Leading to nowhere in a perfectly twisted metaphor
For everything we became
I can't seem to piece together what struck first
I'm still breathing
But I'm still carrying the bruises
Under my skin and the armour I have built

T.S. Curtis

The Little Fairy Tales

Our little fairy tale
Through fairy glades
Through waterfalls
Through heartache
And frozen moments

Petaled hems
Flipping skirts
Edge of all of it

I lie on the bed of thorns
You made for us
If I'm still
The bites I can bear
Perfect still
Perfectly still
Perfect stillness

Rotten

Words shoved back into my mouth
Ghosts of bruises
Still line my lips
Trying to forget
To cover
How does the same love
With gentle hands
And thoughtful gifts
Leave rot behind

T.S. Curtis

Wrong Time

Remember that pact you made me
Said there'd be some kind of always
We'd always have secret handshakes
And all those memories
My friends are your friends and they said
No sides
And good on us

We were always
A me and you
So perfectly gorgeous on the outside
Crying behind my closed door
Shoving feelings back inside
Friends first and lovers last
Who knew we would never last
But we were always right person
Wrong time

I kept the pact
You made me
Said someday it'll be
You and me
You let all of this
Break angry
Cause even right person
Wrong time
Is heartbreak awaiting

And everything
I thought I'd lose is
Already
Gone

A Drive Through the Rubble of Mother Nature's Fury

Green breaks
Where they held the line
Fighting for the lives of the nature
The rest of us quietly destroyed
Pretending to forget the consequences

The burnt trunks
Of ashen birch trees
The ground has started to grow again
Reclaiming
What is rightfully theirs
Like hope amongst the desolate
For life will out

T.S. Curtis

Mourning Sun

Seventeen branches
Scattered over the stairs
Ripped from the comfort of the mother tree
In the mayhem of the middle of the night storm

We complained about the loss of power

They lost everything tonight

St. Sebastian's Place

The Ancients

Hollowed out history
Manicured paths
One signature
For the deaths
Cut
Shredded
A hundred lifetimes
A lifeline
Communications systems
Mother
Rooted in a cosmic world
We will never get to
Be a part of
Until we are buried with her
A hundred lifetimes
Ruined
In thirty seconds

T.S. Curtis

Your Hand

When do I get to stop
Being the one having
To reach out

St. Sebastian's Place

T.S. Curtis

ROOTHEAD

St. Sebastian's Place

T.S. Curtis

Graduate

It's not about walking across the stage

It's about the world that's waiting for you
On the other side

St. Sebastian's Place

Broken door latch
Booze in the air
Overgrown gardens with plants we all forget the names of
And women's weapons forgotten under the window
Sign points the way
To a safe space
Cozy that's not quite home
And doesn't need to be

I sit at a wearing bar
As the band plays forgotten folklore
Masked in alternative rock
And if anyone sings along
The pact you enter into
Isn't one with a face you'll know

The ravine before the bridge
Behind the third tree
Will clean the city grime from your shoes
But leave the rest of you
Because everything is welcome here
The broken
And the beautiful
The impossible
And the *they said being us was wrong*
And the *we know better*

St Seb's place
Is for the misfits
And forgotten travellers
The stories
That have not found their place yet
Who are looking for their people
And themselves

We are the
Patrons

T.S. Curtis

Of the lost bar
And quiet tables
And early nights
And late ones with quiet endings

There's a coat check
For the mask you wear for the world
And lockers
For the persona you've been trying to carry

And behind the bar
His hair done up out of his face
Is Sebastian
Patron Saint of Misfits
And Loners
Reclaimed by our kind
He pours shots of apple juice
To stay the migraines
Of the world
And listens to stories of young women
Who can't bear the weight of what we carry
Any longer
But this is a safe space to just
Be us

There's a couple
Kissing by the door
Zero proof cocktails in hand
All decisions their own
Because we are our own people
History
And bodies be damned
His red lipstick smudged down
Her chin

A fire is crackling
In a fireplace
Each stone
Touched by a memory

St. Sebastian's Place

Each log brought in and swept away like the
Dust of the old faerytales keeping the place alive

You won't find us if you're looking
But St. Seb's kind
Are always ready
To take you in
Because when the world has abandoned you
Saints and the good kind of sinners
And loners too
Any and all are worthy here

T.S. Curtis

I Am Not A Church Pew
(Originally Published in 2019 in Heart & Healing)

I am not a church pew
I am not a place to visit once a week
And pretend you have done a good thing
I am not something you can just ignore
When I do not fit you
I am not comfortable
I am not comfortable with lies between teeth and pages
I may be a religious artifact
But I am in no caught in history
I will not bend under your pressure
No matter how many times you push against me
I have not been stripped raw
My welcoming arms have not cracked
I cannot be used to damn any you see as foul without cause
I am not a church pew
But there a welcome few who've worshipped here

Falling With Grace

I'm happy enough
To be the bigger person
Always backing away
Knowing that to fall into chaos with grace
Is an art
I perfected long ago
That no one deserves to be sucked into
The chaos of whatever this is
I'm the thing people fear
So I've been told
Chased out of the garden of people's lives
But it's in the kindness
And the way I want to be the grace
And the good
But
There was never any way to fall gently into me
Let me show you the art
Of the chaos
I would fall with you
With a smile on my face
Anytime you're ready

T.S. Curtis

Quies

Who knew
My chaos would find tranquility
In the one place where my feet
Never stop moving

St. Sebastian's Place

My Peace

I was chaos
You're peace

You made my dad smile
Your mom always had stories to tell me
Little gifts you said reminded of the little parts of me
Wrapped in little notes of memories and perfect melodies

You were always perfect poetry
All those little things
From the smiles to the way you breathe
Glances across the room that made me feel seen
For the first time in a long while

I was chaos
You're peace

I have derailed
Too many good things
And good people
And I will not put another
Into my path of ruin
No one is ready
To waltz into ruin with me
And I'd never be the one to ask
Always the one to step back

When you're chaos
Needs your peace
Bring me home

T.S. Curtis

Perfect

Someone who eats the pickles
Because I keep rolling them to the edge of my plate
Doesn't even ask just picks them up
Someone who prefers the left side of the bed
So they can slide in beside me already part of my life
Who likes late nights
And a million alarms that I will ultimately sleep through
Someone who knows how I take my tea
But only brings it after asking the offering
Give advice I probably won't take
Offers an arm to walk
Just cause
Shoulder to cry on
And smiles
When they finally get me to laugh

St. Sebastian's Place

A Home For The Next

I started to realize that
I never needed to look for home
In the arms of someone who
Wouldn't even show me to the door
Because my best friend
That kind of best friend
Who no matter how long it goes
Every word and little moment
Feels like coming home
To a door held wide open

To the best friends
Across the world
Whose lives are torn apart
By fate and purpose
Who are the warm hearth
Every time you knock on the door
No matter how long it's been
You know that you'll be seen again

T.S. Curtis

Safe Spaces

I pointed at the window of the first dorm
Where I was falling in love
With someone I was told I shouldn't be
Because she
Wasn't someone who would love me for me

Too many years hiding who I was
Because I was afraid of people I loved
And of myself

Something about a flag in a window
All the colours that have come to mean me
That have come to be part of my identity
Means a little piece of me
Gets to breathe in some kind of healing
Even if I'm ten years removed from that room

Still Here

Cause I will still be here
When she decides
She's over you
And that she's tired of
Some stupid little part of you
And you've taken your sadness out
On me and yelled about how unfair it is
And after weeks of being ignored
Over and over
Left on read
Because I'm just the girl friend
I'll be important enough
For you to text me back
With a life update
Until you agree to your next second date
And I will still be here
Ready to put your pieces back together
The next time
Because I am still here
For you
No matter what

Still Here Pt. 2

But I needed you too
You know

I can't always put you back together
If the pieces I'm trying to put back on me
Are still fresh with glue
I'm still here
But I won't always be if there's nothing left of me

St. Sebastian's Place

Clockwork (Still Here Pt. 3)

Hey

Can you talk?

...

All Those Epic Loves

Every character
I write
Gets an epic love story
The kind of story that defies the odds
The kind of love that survives
In kindness
That isn't about overcoming their faults that hurt you
But letting it be a love
Without hurt

There can be love stories that don't hurt

Not every love poem
Has to be about the struggle
To stay in love
Or the broken loves
Sometimes
The best muse
Is a little bit of joy

My characters get to go on the adventures
I have always been too afraid to say yes to
My epic love story is marred
By anger and words of shame
My characters get epic love stories because
I thought I had mine
And then decided I didn't deserve one anyways

And I am reminding myself that
One Day
I might just get my own soft love story

Sue, Misrule, and Patchouli

When I open your letter
I want to sink into the pages
And hope your ink is enough to embrace me
My darling
I can smell your perfume
Lingering in the pages
And I hold you to my face
There is some part of you here
The closest I can get
As fate has ripped me apart
From my dearest friend
Smudged lines where you always lean onto your page
And the ever-comforting smell of your home
That is just the smiles of your parents
As they make breakfast for whoever is there that day
And I long to be the one there
Laughing into the late nights
And crying into the twilight
Whispering secrets under your covers
Hoping it never ends
This never ends
For now
We are nothing but words
Pen strokes across the country
I can take in every part of you who are
In those pen marks
In the way you wore your perfume as you wrote
And the way the seal you used
Is almost as perfect as you are
Always a perfectionist
My perfect pen pal
There is something so longing and close
About letters
A phone call will never quite match
How I can tell you things here
Hide meanings between my words
And hold a piece of you

T.S. Curtis

Between the notes of jasmine and patchouli
And I know you had that pendant on that you found
At the odd little shop
The thrill and agony of checking the post
Every morning
And every day on the walk home
To see if I get to hold your hand
Where it brushed the page
Left stains that formed your pretty scrawl
Let me drink in your perfume
Still lingering on the pages
And hope that the embrace you've left in the words in your dark purple ink
Are enough to sustain me until you've embraced me again
For real
Now, until next time,
Know I'll let your words linger close to me
Your page at my lips as I ponder your words
The tight hugs that kept me from falling apart
Now, until next time,
Signed,
Yours, *Best Friend*

Fairy Woods

Like flecks off my watercolour brushes
Raindrops sliding across the backs of my hands
Cold enough for my breathing to leave question marks behind on the air
It's not a sad grey sky like the poets would tell you
It's home
Bright grey that blankets everything
The cold warmth wrapped over the world's shoulders
Lets you appreciate every other colour against the blank canvas
The rain has left the world perfectly still
Too chilly for your neighbours
But not us
This is part of us
Trees bowing to us
Lingering green whispering stories in the breeze
Black squirrel and raven peering from their roosts
The warm hearth inside
Promise of tea
Fairy lit path to a borrowed home
That feels more home than some I've called my own

T.S. Curtis

Putting Down Tracks

There's a path through the woods
Behind my house
I went round and round the loop
For years at a time
Hoping to come out
More me
Than where I started

There's still remnants
Of my walks
Where I left my mark on the yellow bridge
And my footprints buried
Under the stories of others finding
Their peace
And I'm still looking for the exactness of mine

Saying goodbye
To the little pieces of a walkway
That became as much home
And an escape
And a kind of church
As everything else in a town
I spent two decades
Looking for me in

There's a path through the woods
Across the highway from my new home
Some things change
Some things stay the same
I'm putting on my backpack and my hiking boots
And I hope to find myself
At the end of this loop

St. Sebastian's Place

It's Okay To Be An Ending

Sometimes love ends with
A smile at the edge of a dinner table
Wishing our hands could have brushed
And if that spark would be enough
In my favourite lipstick
That you said made my smile brighter
And I caught you looking longer as you played
For our conversation
And the hesitation in wanting to ask a question
And I let the love die
First at a dinner table
And then in a spotlight
Where you were your happiest
And I remembered my path was far away
And even if we could be an us
It would never be the best us
And I let it be that way
But I still smile at your photo
The way you used to smile at me across the crowded room when you thought I wasn't watching

T.S. Curtis

Mending (or: Blurry October)

I hugged your mom today
Because after every shard you shoved into my heart
And her fingers dug into the fissures you made
I know what it's like to break

St. Sebastian's Place

The Recovering Memory

My body remembers
The way I mistreated it
The hurtful days
Still linger under my skin
It's swallowed back the scars
I left on it
Thankfully I'm the only one who has to remember
What I went through

My body will show
The way I handled recovery
Scars of the days I fell from climbing walls
As I reached further than my skills
And my muscles will hate me the next morning
But my memories will hold on to how good it felt to try
The stretches of my body being given the chance
To survive
To thrive
Because I stopped hating myself
Your words will not leave scars behind
I have outgrown
Your ability to ruin me

This road to recovery
Has been littered with the potholes
And pitfalls
Of my own hatred
I skinned my knees
On the pavement
Falling to get back to the ways I wanted to be

But we were always built to be resilient

We are built to mend

This is a body
Grown and built and shaped in love

T.S. Curtis

Who cares what it is that it looks like

St. Sebastian's Place

For The Broken Little Girls

When the day comes
That you decide
There is something about the world
And you
That matters
And you stop lashing at the gentle fingers
And the world gets to see
The sharp edges
And the way you put yourself back together
And the harsh words
You turned on the world
Because you don't want them turned on you
Start to come back
We won't blame you
Because we *know*

We have been there
We are the scars
Of the broken edges
We have stitched back together
On our own
And in a community

The broken girls
That kept me together
Were sewn together with the kind words
Of another
Good words
And stupid quotes
And silly jokes
Passed through generations of broken girls
That keep us going
So that broken girls
Become Strong Women
And when you are ready to join us

We are here

T.S. Curtis

Why I Stopped Caring What Others Said

I have the face of my
Great-grandmother

And in buckets of old photographs
No one is sure if it's my great aunt
Or me
A constant reminder
Of generations that have survived
To bring me a better life

I have my dad's chin
And his eyes
And I know everything he sacrificed
And the people he endured

I have my dad's hands
Gentle and delicate
Creating when the world gets too loud

I have my mom's voice
And the cadence that has soothed half a generation
In a place we were mad to call hometown
That wreaked havoc on the body

I share my sister's determination
And have found my own way
To be strong enough to hold her up

I have my sister's temper
And the fire behind our eyes
When something isn't right
Or the anger boils over
Matches to a tee
And even when she felt like she was slipping through my fingers
Rage at a broken world always brought us back together

I have my sister's face

St. Sebastian's Place

Same perfect cheeks
That I hated myself for
But always loved on her
And could never truly reconcile how that could be
Her and I were two halves
Of one person
How could I hate that

I have a body the ancestors could only dream about
And am coded from thousands of years of survival
Family lines
And cultures
Coming together
And I forgot to honour who they were
To fit who I thought this place wanted me to be
I don't need to be
Anyone
But who the people who have my back
Made me to be

T.S. Curtis

Why I Am More Careful With What I Say

Every time
My mother said there was something wrong
With her beautiful self
I stood in front of the mirror
And wondered if I
Too
Wasn't good enough
Because her body
Built mine
And in my eyes
She was perfect

And I look like my sister
Our hair and eyes don't match
But everything else does
Down to the way the fire builds
And flashes over
Hot and angry and trouble-causing
And some day she could turn me into Tante

    And that means they could look like me
    And they deserve to know that the woman they came from
                                                     is beautiful
    And the people they will become will always
                                       without fail
    Be beautiful

There are ears around me all the time
I watched two girls stand in front of a mirror
In a quiet living room
Trying to decide if they shouldn't tuck their shirts in
Because they were worried it made their hips stick out
And I remember the days of doing the same
And putting those words in the mouths of little girls who have not even seen the world yet
Broke my heart

St. Sebastian's Place

Over
And over
There is something prepped in a media queue to tell us some piece of us is ready to be removed
Innovation is catching up to the words they sell on the newspaper stand
You can remove something as fast as grabbing lunch with friends
Every fifth scroll
Reminds that
The body of each person is different
But somehow the sixth post
Tells them only a third of those bodies
Are worthy of love

Every one of them
Is worthy of love
Every part of them is created with tender beauty

My mouth runs a mile a minute
And my brain hated every part of me
And in a dangerous combination
I was outside and inside of the terror of hatred
And the world got to know my pain with me
Sometimes quietly
Subtly
Dropped just enough you had to listen to notice
Sometimes
Loud enough that I scared even myself

I am balancing my words
And I may not love every piece
But I am trying
Because the next person who has ears to listen
Will know that being
Is being
Is being what you are meant to be

T.S. Curtis

Lips Moving

Out of synch
Because I haven't been able to
Hear the perfect pitch
Of my sister's best laugh
In years
And I still resist the urge to
Throw my phone at the wall when I realize
No, it does not go any louder
My world went quiet
And I thought my voice would go with it
I think in a whole new way
My thoughts can be seen in the world before you
Hands and fingers moving as I work through
The tidbits of detail your lips have left behind
I feel the world through my fingertips
It may not be the same
But it became the best stand in
And my hands moving are not a nervous tick
Or an annoying habit
You can stop my hands from moving
Or try to call me out and make me feel embarrassed
As many times as you wish
The reality is
My hands opened the doors
To a community who welcomed
A terrified little girl with open arms
Your lips move
I still know what you're saying
My hands move
You decided you were lost

St. Sebastian's Place

You Did Not Manifest This, I Promise

I said once my broken body
Was the cruel joke ripped straight from the pages of a poem
A broken soul
Finding its way to the surface
Demanding the world know
What I had done
What they had done
What he had done

You did not cause it

I promise

This body is still broken
But it is controlled
It moves with intention and there are days
When it rests
This soul is not broken
It has been mended
Needle and thread
Tape and glue
And a thumbtack or two
And in the end
Inside and out
We'll be okay
Because cracks can be mended
In whatever way we decide is best

T.S. Curtis

THE CANON

St. Sebastian's Place

T.S. Curtis

The Saints of This Place

Into the woods I go
To find my mind
Rebuild my soul

With patron Saints
Of all good things
Through ye olde
And the new
Worlds
Gathering place of protection
And altered stories
Missed missives
Canon fodder
Broken memories
Harsh endings

With accidental Saints
Who build the good
Somewhere quietly

To be a saint
Of this place
Is to be all that you are
For the good of all of the rest
Leave it all up to fate

St. Sebastian's Place

Abandoned Place of Worship

I am an
Abandoned place of worship
No pious visitors
No naysayers at the door

The canon placed
Boundaries and rules
Laid like the worn carpet of an alter
Waiting for congregants
To relight the candles
All blown out
Wind in cracked windows
Abandoned church pews
Cracked hardwood

A welcome few
Make pilgrimage
Worshipped here
Down on your knees
Like a prayer

Pained penance

Rebirth below the surface

Abandoned place of worship
Cracked pews
And yellowed pages
Holy water anointing the birds
Bring word to the flocks
Until the candles are lit again
And one day
The light always comes back

T.S. Curtis

Historical Notes

Sweet Sebastian
A perfect gentleman
Sharp cheeks
For a red carpet
Kind eyes

Persecuted for your love
Of a loving God
Beliefs twisted
Forged in a new world

Little known
But from your writers
Milanese traveller
Sins against an emperor
Soft mouth
Sharp words

Twice a martyr
Raised on a tree
Shot
Filled with arrows
As though an Urchin
Left for dead

Rescued by the Widow
Whose gentle hands spun healing
Brought back from the brink
To spread the word
The word of good
Of love
Say freely
Beaten
For protecting the oppressed
Left in the sludge

St. Sebastian's Place

To protect the Unprotected
The disabled
And the sick
A protector against plague
And the soldiers of battles external
And internal

The beautiful man
And protector
A homecoming
For the beaten
The damned
For the battles too heavy to bear alone
The words that slice like arrows
Bury in the skin
Mark the sinners
By their standards
Before the world is ready to be in step
With the different
And then new
For our love of one another
A reminder that kindness
Goodness
Belief
Self and the creator
Is the best thing to have
Kind hands for those lost
Tied to trees
And fence posts
Destroyed for a love
A belief
When the nastiness seeps in
We are stronger than

T.S. Curtis

Until Safer Tides

St. James
Protector of the wayfarers
In boats on treacherous seas
We were only meant to be
but Simple Fishers
Catch and release
Calm seas
Homemade nets holding together old wounds
Patched vessels taking us across our journey

St. James
Breathe safety onto those
Braving their battles
In the growing swells
Of their own personal perilous seas
Keep watch over those of us who will keep swimming
But start to wonder
If swimming in circles
Is truly worth whatever alleged journey
We have been told we are resilient enough to brave

Storming seas
The swirls of clouds
We used to point out when the shores
Still felt like the safety of home
Before we felt pulled in the wrong direction
Before they pulled us under
St. James
I can't breathe
These are not the soft days
Of grey skies
And grey waters
And churning waves
The white caps keep pulling me under

I can't breathe

St. Sebastian's Place

St. James
Protector of the fisherman
Still finding their way
The journeys of bravery and
Pilgrimages into
Ourselves

Until
St. James
Be the peace
May we be comforted
In the belief that our calmer seas
Are coming
For the evening's red sky
Is not a warning
But a promise
That safer tides
Be on their way
Dear travellers

Chin up
Our calmer seas are coming

T.S. Curtis

Softly (An Ode to St. Francis)

Go softly
Let the Good News
Move you
Keep your face
Towards the sun

Go softly
The smallest of our world
Shivers of cat whiskers
Whisper of wings
Sea breeze and scurrying crabs

Go softly
See the good
In the world
In the people
Don't let
Then disappear
Through the cracks

Go softly
Give freely
For the love of the world
For the love of all things
For the love of yourself
Go softly

St. Sebastian's Place

St. Atwood

Prophetess
Storyteller

The stories we know
The stories we don't
What we include
All the things we leave out
When the stories are made
Who the stories will hold
Hold the past gently
Keep the edges from crumbling
To hold the past
Is to write the future
Prophets
And storytellers
Are only so far apart

August

Sweet pear
Plucked from a neighbour tree
Dribbling down my chin
In early fall heat
Out of season

Bright sun
Blinding warmth
Tell me the ways of your world
Give the philosophers
Fodder
In our hazy days
Perfect memories
Created in the little subverts
St. Augustine's children
Making merry
Drunk on pears
Confessing our sins
Some that have yet to pass

St. Sebastian's Place

Joan's Girls

Raise your sword
Our dragons did not come
Breathing fire

Wielding

Joan's girls
Sharp of tongue
Raise your words
Like a glass of wine
To spill
Stain
On their shirts
And reputations
Let them hear the voices
As blood spills
Blood chilling
Our control
Our body
Our country
Fight for what
Has always been right
Strong girls
Lipstick chainmail
Hold strong her mantle

Blasphemous girls
Heresy in the screams for justice
To hold the deeds to our own bodies
In the refusal to submit quietly

Joan's girls
Raise the sword
Sharpen your words
Defenders of ourselves
And each other
They cannot burn us all

T.S. Curtis

St. Gobnait

St. Gobnait of the impossible
A buzz of all life
Our lifelines
At the bottom of all
Life grown
Rising from the soil
First reminder
Of spring
A body that should never get off the ground
Wings too small
Do the impossible
When the rules say
It can never be done
Let your spirit
Their buzz
Bring you back to life

St. Rita

I found my saint
Buried in a library
Her nose in a book

The lost cause
Of a broken-hearted girl
Too many times to count
Bruises no one will ever see
St. Rita
Please heal me
Mend the cracks inside
Soothe the wounds
Inflicted in his perfected values
A millennia of perfect words

Safe corners
Lost in books
Rose perfume
To calm the senses
It's a lost cause
This broken girl

Who may just need a hug
And a friend's sharp word
Show the door
No lost causes
Here are the happily ever afters

T.S. Curtis

The Miller

Grinding down the coarse
Memories
And heartbreak
And nitpicking ways
For the soft end of becoming

Leader of the Wild Girls
Where memories grow
Even with the bruises

Gentle fingers
Gentle strains
Soft smiles
Dance in summer rain
Race under trees
Small signs
With old dedications

No need to yearn
For validation
Here you are safe
Everything will be okay
Be everything you are
You will never be too much
In the quiet
And the tears
The love here
Will never
Go away
I will never
Go away
I promise

Honest words
Faltering in old hurt
Every sacred feeling
Is soft here

St. Sebastian's Place

You're always wanted
Here
Adventures planned
The rubble of the old wounds
A place to build a path back to yourself

Reeling from the burns
The footprints left behind
In salt water
Ready for new adventures
You are braver than you believe
In the gentle hands
Of The Miller
Picking up
And treating new
Everything will be
Okay
Again

T.S. Curtis

Little Girl, Bloodied Fingers

This is not a ghost story
Not pulled from pages
Nor passed through the camp flame

This is not a ghost story

Blood drips from where
She tore herself apart

Little girl
Bloodied fingers
Destroying the last of everything you were

Blood-soaked words
This is no fantasy
No horror story
This is the future
And it will heal itself
With time

St. Sebastian's Place

The Robin

The girl of many names
Blue eyed possibility
Safe place
To land
Leave stories
And secrets

Leave the struggle at the door
Slip into who you are
Find the comfort in the letters
In the words
In the prefix
In the history
You will always
Be the best version of you
It's okay to hide
Keep the layers safe
Hold it beneath your coat
But don't keep it forever
You are an inspiration to all the others
Who may come behind you
Being you
Is better
Than all the roles you will try to play

T.S. Curtis

To Love Again

Lovers
Pulled apart
Across the world
In desire
Of their bettering
Skyspanse keeping
Them in their worlds
St. Valentine
Protect the love
Keep it safe
A world
Tries to pull the good things
St. Valentine
Old beliefs
Twisted with decades
Centuries
Rewritten
Love poems
Love letters
Love notes
Left in heart holes
Keep this heart whole
St. Valentine
Leave your strength
Your sight
Hindsight is 20/20
Let the small fights
Mean nothing
Lover
Hold tight
Keep fast
There's a world
For us to see

St. Isidore

Buzz of life
As words flow through my pen.
St. Isidore
Guide my hand,
Make my words strong
to share these stories.
St. Isidore
Proofread my wallows
The leave my fears
The hurt
On the page.
Continuing tradition
of the poets who have come before,
Do not let my words waver
Leave me strength
To drain the poison
Stop the aching
Break the mold.
St. Isidore
Keep me upright
To tell the stories
Wrap in the metaphors
Until day breaks
On what I can leave behind

Full stop.

T.S. Curtis

Lament to St. Lidwina

Shed my skin and bones
This body
Is not a temple
This body is no home
Dust filled breaths
Chest squeezed
Blood boiling
On cool spring days
Bruised fingers
Swollen knuckles
Cobwebbed eyes
No songs to pluck out
No lessons left
In this pain
Burning cords
Up the spine
Down the spine
Around the line
Of every limb
Tight twists
Stuck steps
Every second
Every moment
Something flares
In the pain
On a scale of one to ten
That keeps changing the goal post
If last week was a ten
How are we here again
And beyond
Ravaged body
Unseen harm
Day after day
Breath after breath
Maybe one day
I will get my life in abundance

St. Sebastian's Place

Disclaimer,

This is to tell you that
Sometimes the world closes in on us
And we look back
To realize all the pieces we had missed
And try to piece them back together
Sometimes
It isn't as pretty as we had hoped
And days sitting in a chair
Talking it through
Feels like it might just be making it unravel
But words
Can weave it back into place
Or at least into something manageable
If it is your first book
Or your fourth try piecing together the story
Take all the time you need
To feel you are complete

St. Sebastian's Place

T.S. Curtis

And now
It is your turn
Turn the page
To write along with me, and add your own words into the walls of
St. Sebastian's Place

St. Sebastian's Place

T.S. Curtis

Write a poem to someone who hurt you so deeply you never wanted to forgive them. Let out all the anger.

*Now **forgive** them. (Not for them: for yourself, in whatever those words look like)*

What does coming home mean to you? Is it a place? A person? A moment?

St. Sebastian's Place

*Take this book with you to your favourite place outdoors. Choose to either write to describe what you see, or go beyond and write a poem **to** that place.*

T.S. Curtis

St. Sebastian's Place

T.S. Curtis

- Author's Note -

St. Sebastian was an early Christian, martyred for his beliefs. If you are looking for him in iconography, he is typically depicted tied up and shot with arrows – but surviving the blows. Sometimes, he is tied to a tree, sometimes he is tied to a column. His story is one that is told through themes of defiance, being broken but continuing, nonetheless. He was shot by arrows and is said to have been the only survivor during a mass execution, then nursed back to health by a woman who would become another Saint. He is the patron saint of soldiers, athletes, people with disabilities, numerous cities in different countries across the world quietly tying them together with an invisible, faithful string. And somewhere, along the way, he accidentally became the patron saint of queer people. A gay icon. The origin for this varies depending on who you talk to: the first time I heard about him in this way, in a Religion and Sexuality course, it was tied to the iconography in which he is depicted – lithe, muscular body, slightly *homoerotic* posing (leave it to the Renaissance and Romantic painters). But others say, and I think I lean somewhat towards this, that it was just how many queer people connected to his story. Beaten down for being different. An identity that was outlawed. Literally struck with arrow after arrow, physical manifestations of the thing they are trying to break from you, in you, and a physical show of the people, the hurtful words that strike. (Despite common belief, there are religious queer people, and there are many affirming churches as well – I grew up in one.)

Taking St. Seb, and combining him with the vibe of a real St.-named bar I once stumbled into that felt like something out of a dream, gave me what felt like the perfect title and titular poem for this collection.

Like I said, religion was a part of my upbringing – my elementary and junior high school was a French Catholic school and while I don't need to get too far into that lore, it did give me a really deep interest in Angel lore, and the lore of the Saints. I spent a good year or two really obsessed with some of the more obscure Saints, trying to understand how that worked. I was not Catholic, but formed a lot by what I learned from them (good and bad). During the pandemic, I came back around to faith, trying to understand where I stood, what I believed, and honestly I still don't really know, but I did get back into the learning side and just consumed everything I could. I wrote a couple pieces referencing Saints in different ways – if I remember correctly, St. James was the first "saint" poem I played around with. I think there was something comforting about believing in this way, both before and during the pandemic when a lot of my life felt like it was out of control, falling apart. Then it became an exploration of what saint meant, how they get canonized. That got even more solidified when I took a course on Margaret Atwood's novels and was introduced to her Maddaddam trilogy, in which names we recognize show up as Saints in this post-apocalyptic world Atwood has created.

I initially described the vibe of this collection to someone as "angry girl with religious trauma trying to heal in the woods." Take that as you will. Anger felt like the root.

But they came back with a better word:

Reactionary. The reaction poems.

I had written the broken poems. And the love poems. And the healing poems. This was new. The poems I write are always a reaction to something, but these were reactionary, they were pent up, and angry, and more than a getting out of an emotion.

St. Seb's Place started just before the pandemic of 2020. I was about 15 poems in when suddenly I found myself moving home, to my hometown and the house I had grown up in. And I finished the collection as I emerged from everything and moved on to the next part of my life. It is a collection of growth. I started this collection freshly 20, just barely into my adulthood, if we can even truly call it that. I finished the edits with responsibilities beyond my wildest dreams and actually, in some ways, feeling like a grown up, and a lot of that is reflected in some of these words. Growing up also started to give me the chance to reflect on a lot of things.

This book has a lot of conversations. With other works of literature, art, history, I got experimental with how I wrote poetry, with my own style, had conversations with myself, too. My old self, my old work. The collection has conversations with H&H, Shades of Blue, and Let Them Stare. See if you can spot any of the references. One of my proof copies of St. Seb's is fully marked with all the references I make, and it felt cool to see how I pushed myself artistically.

I completed my 5th Poetry Book while I edited this and pondered it. I had originally planned to put St. Seb's out in 2023 but a mix of anxiety and someone putting my poems and the book down, convinced me not to put it out. As I write this letter to you tucked into book 4, before this 4th is even yours, I have number 5 starting to feel beautiful. The next place to dump the words I was too afraid to say for so long, dragging them out of the depths of journals and notebooks. I'm very proud of it. Working on it, though, while cleaning this up, finishing it, is interesting. To watch and feel how different they are and how they – the words, but also the girl who wrote them – deal with things so differently, yet so similarly too.

Welcome to St. Sebastian's place. Stay as long as you need. See you in the next one <3

- Acknowledgements -

Acknowledgements as an indie are tough, at times. This section is meant for the people in our life, and that should often involve the people who brought the physical book part of this together. However, I am a one-woman show, from writing, to formatting, to the cover photo. So a quick thank you to me – for surviving the things that led to the poems, for hiking until I got the right photos for the cover, for spending hours writing, editing, and designing.

To my coffee maker, which sustained me through many late night editing sessions.

To my mom, as always, who reads anything I send and gives me her fully honest critique even when I would probably prefer at least five minutes of coddling.

To my sister, Solveig. This book is dedicated to her because when I took a step back, looked at everything I had written, thought about the time when I had started it and worked hard on it in our parents' basement in the height of that "we all have to be indoors" time, she was the person who got me through. Wiped my tears, picked me up, convinced me I was strong enough to keep going, got angry with me when I needed it. She seriously considered beating someone up for me. It was what I needed and even if she forgets how to answer the phone 5 to 17 times a week, she is the rock I need in my life, and the best part of it.

To my Ottawa crew. You know who you are, and you may or may not know what you helped get me through. Some of you were there for it, and some of you were there for the after. Holding my hand, finding old broken pieces and helping fit them back into place. For supporting my writing, being sent prototypes and drafts, and checking in. Being extra eyes on the book and catching spelling mistakes.

To Robyn. So that your name is in print and you are seen, and you know that every piece of you is important.

To Sarah and Jade for breathing life back into me, listening to whatever was on my mind, and being there after the weeks when I was too busy to be a good friend.

To Lisa Handley who when I left home for the third time in my life felt like a safe place to land. For giving me opportunities, feedback, and support at every turn, making me a better educator, and person.

To M, for putting up with me dragging them on a full-blown hike to get photos for the cover.

And to MM. For basically everything at this point. From falling apart to great adventures. Thank you for reminding me how easy friendships can be.

- About the Author -

T.S. Curtis is a writer who cannot claim on genre as her own, finding a love of writing in poetry which was where she started to find her confidence, thanks to a mentor, but her first love was fiction in fantasy, contemporary fiction, and dystopian genres. Born and raised in northern Alberta, Canada, T.S. can't decide what part of Canada feels like home. She spent her high school years on Vancouver Island, and moved to Ottawa, Ontario, to pursue a degree in History and Political Science, and has recently found herself back on the Island. She started university as a business student, but quickly realized it was absolutely not the type of things she wanted to be learning – and since switching, she has become a big advocate of making mistakes and finding your path at your own pace. She has worked in restaurants, hotels, tour guiding, government offices, and is now pursuing working in secondary education. All the while, writing stayed her beloved, passion project on the side. Her two favourite things in the whole world are her two black cats.

Outside of writing and education, T.S.' great loves include dance, reading every fantasy and dystopian book she can get her hands on, rock climbing and boxing, singing along badly to musicals, and being outside. One of her biggest goals in life is to visit every province and territory in Canada, every national park, and as many strange and cool restaurants as she possibly can.

She can be found most social medias at **@TSC_WIP**, on Goodreads at **T.S. Curtis**, and on her beloved website and blog **tscurtis.com**.

T.S. Curtis

St. Sebastian's Place

T.S. Curtis

St. Sebastian's Place

www.ingramcontent.com/pod-product-compliance
Lightning Source LLC
LaVergne TN
LVHW092051080525
810749LV00005B/593